Original title:
The House on the Edge of Tomorrow

Copyright © 2025 Creative Arts Management OÜ
All rights reserved.

Author: Jaxon Kingsley
ISBN HARDBACK: 978-1-80587-222-1
ISBN PAPERBACK: 978-1-80587-692-2

Tides of Time's Relentless Flow

Waves of time come crashing in,
Tick-tock, where has the day been?
I tripped on moments, slipped on cheer,
Laughing at clocks, oh dear, oh dear!

Sandy toes and sunny frowns,
Time shuffles in mismatched gowns.
It dances wild, a slippery ghost,
Saying, 'Catch me if you can, you host!'

In the Shadow of Tomorrow's Dreams

Tomorrow peeks with a cheeky grin,
'What's new?' it asks, 'Did you begin?'
Stumbling over hope's bright strings,
   Chasing after the joy it brings.

Dreams poke fun, they jump and sway,
  While I'm stuck in yesterday's play.
  They giggle as I try to keep pace,
   With fortune hiding in a silly race!

Where Forgotten Futures Ruminate

Once I planned a grand parade,
But forgot the map, oh what a trade!
Dancing with shadows, lost in thought,
Where's that big future I once sought?

The future lurks in strange old shoes,
Wearing mismatched socks, spreading news.
It mocks me gently, but that's just fine,
I'll join its dance, sipping on time's wine!

Cracks in Reality's Fabric

Reality's fabric has a tear,
Where squirrels plan world domination, I swear!
They giggle and chatter on treetop thrones,
While I try to find my lost hair comb.

These cracks let in a wacky breeze,
Whirling thoughts that aim to tease.
Upside-down is the new right-side-up,
As I sip from an invisible cup!

Glistening Moments on the Horizon

In a kitchen bright with flair,
A cat is plotting, unaware.
The toast pops up, a frantic dance,
While butter leaps in a dizzy trance.

A parrot mocks with silly sounds,
As cereal spills all around.
Each crack of dawn brings laughter loud,
In this joyful chaos, I'm so proud.

Between Yesterday and the Unknown

A sock is missing, oh what fun,
Detached from pairs like a lost run.
The fridge hums tunes of yesteryear,
While pickles pirouette with cheer.

Old photos grin in goofy poses,
Reminders of life's stinky roses.
Each memory's a story spun,
A dance with time that can't be undone.

Where Dust Dances with Time

Dust bunnies form a leafy trail,
These little critters will prevail.
They twirl and spin like tiny sprites,
In corners sly, they host their rites.

With each sweeping motion, they play,
In the sunlight's glow, they sway.
Laughter fills the air so light,
As they tango through the night.

Reflections in a Glistening Pane

The glass reflects a face so strange,
A wild hairdo, a little change.
I grin at my quirky charm today,
A joyful mess in every way.

Outside, squirrels have a nutty race,
While I break into a silly face.
With every glance, there's pure delight,
In this comedic morning light.

Halls of Memory and Desire

In corridors of lost dreams light,
Where socks and laughter take their flight.
The cat plays chess with ghosts at noon,
As dust bunnies plot to rule the room.

A teapot sings a tune of cheer,
While old shoes dance, defying fear.
The fridge is a portal to delight,
With leftovers that dare to take flight.

In the Echoes of Faded Walls

Whispers flirt in corners damp,
Where memories twirl like a romping lamp.
The wallpaper peels, but so what?
It's just a style that I forgot.

With every creak, the house does laugh,
As chairs tell tales of a silly gaffe.
The echoes giggle, tickling time,
In a symphony of chimes that rhyme.

Floors that Hold Tomorrow's Secrets

Beneath the floorboards, stories sleep,
As mice hold meetings, their secrets keep.
The carpet's worn but full of grace,
It trips the unwary with a smiley face.

A dance recital for brave and bold,
As furniture plays, breaking the mold.
Every squeaky step, a stampede of fun,
In a riddle home where joy's never done.

Beneath the Old Oak's Whisper

Under branches that gossip and sway,
Lies a picnic where ants join the fray.
With sandwiches that never get old,
A feast of laughter, a sight to behold.

The breeze tells jokes, making leaves giggle,
As shadows do a silly little wiggle.
Beneath this tree, time takes a break,
Where fun grows wild like a sweet cupcake.

The Liminal Space of Becoming.

In a hallway with mismatched shoes,
Two cats debate, sipping on their brews.
An old clock winks with a mischievous chime,
As I trip over yesterday, lost in time.

Jumping through puddles of thought and of whim,
A dance with the shadows, the lights are dim.
A potato in the corner gives me a grin,
Saying, 'Life's much funnier when chaos begins!'

Whispers of a Future Unseen

A toaster talks secrets with a partially burnt slice,
While a blender dreams loudly of mixing up dice.
The curtains gossip about who'll drop by,
As the vacuum hums tunes that make windows sigh.

In the kitchen, a fridge keeps the drinks icy cold,
While the pantry holds stories that never get told.
A dance of the teaspoons, a raucous ballet,
In this silent ensemble, the spoons lead the way.

Shadows Behind the Broken Door

Behind the door where the shadows collide,
A sock puppet mutters, 'Oh, let's take a ride!'
With mismatched companions and head full of dreams,
We'll navigate hiccups and giggle at schemes.

An old broom whispers secrets to dust,
While a lamp sings soft tunes, it's a must.
Here laughter is scattered, like crumbs on the floor,
As we juggle our hopes through the creaky floor.

Dreams on the Precipice of Dawn

In the twilight, when dreams start to mix,
A frog in a top hat performs flashy tricks.
The moon smiles wide, with a wink and a nod,
As I chase after giggles that seem so odd.

With slippers that squeak, I leap for the light,
A dance in pajamas feels perfectly right.
Tomorrow is silly, all wrapped up in cheer,
As I trip into sunlight, banishing fear.

Chasing Shadows Through Open Doors

In a home where laughter trails,
The fridge is stocked with cheese and fails.
Cats play tag with shadows bright,
While we dance like fools at night.

Socks on hands, we gesture wide,
Shrieking as we slip and slide.
A chair becomes a rocket ship,
With cushions on our weird long trip.

The clock ticks slow, a turtle's race,
We plan grand feasts in this small space.
Each corner hides a silly tale,
Of goofy antics that prevail.

Tomorrow's chores can wait, you see,
Let's wear our hats and climb a tree.
Coffee spills, but who needs grace?
In this fun house, we found our place.

A Tapestry of Unlived Life

In a room of echoes, dreams unwind,
Stories linger, one of a kind.
Pickle jars and socks galore,
This could be so much more!

Interviews with dust bunnies rise,
Each one tells its own surprise.
We sit and plot a heist for pie,
While arguing if we could fly.

With couches as our cherished throne,
We rule a kingdom made of foam.
A pizza box, a treasure chest,
In our hands, we are the best.

What if tomorrow's sun won't shine?
We'll wear our shades, look mighty fine.
In this quilt of joy and jest,
We live our lives, we feel so blessed.

Frayed Edges of Tomorrow's Fabric

Threads of laughter, woven tight,
Cereal spills in morning light.
Chasing squirrels dressed in bow ties,
We question if they're secretly wise.

Gardens sprout weeds with a cheer,
We declare them pets, oh dear!
Pitching tents inside the hall,
Every giggle echoes tall.

Board games turn to epic lore,
Dice roll wild, we plead for more.
Days blend like a jelly mix,
Who needs a plan? Just pull a trick!

In shadows long, we find our gaps,
We surf the air and fall in laps.
With frayed edges, we dance and spin,
In this merry chaos, we always win.

The Music of Unsung Journeys

A jester danced on a windy peak,
With shoes that squeaked and a wink so cheeky.
He spun tales of ships that made no splash,
While ducks in bowler hats dashed off to bash.

A symphony played from a grapevine's twist,
Songs of adventures that never quite exist.
With laughter that echoed through the trees,
Even the squirrels paused, feeling the tease.

An Odyssey Beyond What Was

A pirate of old rode a bicycle fleet,
With a parrot who only liked to eat beet.
They searched for treasures in jars of jam,
While reading maps drawn by a talking clam.

Their ship made of cardboard sailed far away,
To lands where Mondays were turned into play.
With mermaids giggling and trolls doing flips,
They hoarded their gold in potato chip dips.

Veil of Tomorrow's Secrets

A wizard in slippers brewed tea with glee,
While mixing potions that bubbled like sea.
He claimed to foresee a pancake parade,
Where syrupy unicorns danced unafraid.

Invisibility cloaks that itched like mad,
Transforming into cats—oh, how they had!
Each whisker tickled with the future's delight,
As fish on bicycles zoomed out of sight.

Footprints on a Future Path

Footprints made of jelly adorned the trail,
Leading to places where moose tell a tale.
They giggle and bounce under colorful skies,
While shadows do the tango—what a surprise!

Cars that honk laughter roll down the street,
With cupcakes as tires, life can't be beat.
Signposts that jiggle and dance with each step,
Whispering secrets in a funny old prep.

Steps into Unwritten Chapters

In a nook where echoes play,
Socks go missing, it's said to stay.
Bouncing ideas off the walls,
Laughter slips through the halls.

Curious cats on missions roam,
Claiming every box as home.
Each corner hides a quirky tale,
Like a never-ending snail mail.

With a spoonful of sugar, dreams ignite,
Potatoes dancing, what a sight!
Imagination flies on a whim,
While the clock ticks, we take a swim.

In this realm where stardust brews,
Chasing after bizarre hues.
We write our saga, puffed with fun,
Underneath the radiant sun.

The Threshold of Endless Possibility

Step right up, let's play a game,
Guess which room has the most fame?
The kitchen sings and pots take flight,
While the fridge hums tunes at night.

In the hallway, mirrors clash and clash,
Reflecting laughter with a splash.
A leap of faith through paint-splattered doors,
Adventure waits; what's in store?

Each step a quirk, each corner a cheer,
A tangle of tales whispers near.
With each laugh, a new path unfurls,
In this land of nonsense, joy twirls.

So gather 'round, friends, and let's dance,
In this surreal, vibrant expanse.
Every moment, a secret to find,
In the realm of the wonderfully blind.

A Roof Above the Uncharted

Under a roof where giggles reside,
Wobbly chairs take a joyride.
Jars of jelly wiggle with glee,
Silly shadows that run free.

In the attic, stories act up,
With dust bunnies jumping and hiccup.
The ceiling's a canvas for thoughts to bloom,
Making magic in every room.

Polka-dotted cushions cuddle so tight,
Until pillows decide to take flight.
Here, the walls wear outfits bright,
As curtains twirl, dancing in light.

So come along, let's weave a song,
In this space where we belong.
Breathless moments, stacking up high,
With laughter that shouts to the sky.

Secrets Beneath the Creaking Floor

Listen close to the floor's big sighs,
Whispers of socks and half-eaten pies.
The wooden planks hold stories old,
Of mischief and dreams, bravely bold.

Beneath the cracks, a world awaits,
Where jellybeans dance with squeaky mates.
The cat's outsmarting the vacuum's roar,
Savoring life on a hidden floor.

Faint giggles echo with every step,
As secrets unfold with each misstep.
Here every shadow holds a clue,
To past adventures waiting for you.

So skip along and don't be shy,
In this space, the weirdest can fly.
Let the creaks and snaps set you free,
In a wonderland of jubilee.

Dusty Portraits of What Lies Ahead

A painting hung, with colors bright,
It laughed at dreams that took to flight.
In a frame of gold, it winks and grins,
Glimpses of futures, where chaos spins.

Old shoes by the door, they tell a tale,
Of journeys embarked, of breezes that sail.
They sit and gather dust, but oh, how they sprout,
With every new choice, there's laughter about.

A cat in a hat, holding a tea,
Predicts the weather—just wait and see!
With each tick-tock, the clock does say,
Let's twirl our fate, in a whimsical way.

And so we dance, with socks mismatched,
In a haphazard waltz, our paths detached.
Through walls worn thin, we share a chuckle,
At portraits of futures, all in a shuffle.

A Symphony of Tomorrow's Echoes

A symphony plays, oh what a sight,
With violins screeching, and cellos in flight.
The future hums a quirky tune,
Beneath the bright and laughing moon.

Ducks in a row, they waddle and quack,
Announcing the rhythm as they lead the pack.
Piano keys tinkle, like bubbles in air,
Each note a mistake that fills us with flair.

A trumpet blares, and the neighbors yell,
At our crazy concert, can't you tell?
With each misplaced beat, we laugh out loud,
In a foolish union, feeling proud.

So grab a spoon, make it your stick,
Join the parade—it's a funny trick.
In this joyous chaos, let's all be free,
And dance to echoes of what will be!

Sails Against a Brisk Horizon

Sails billow brightly, as winds do spin,
Chasing the sun with a cheeky grin.
Waves have a secret, they bubble and bounce,
Drawing us in, just watch as they flounce.

A compass that spins, it points to a jest,
Where pirates are holding a treasure chest.
"X" marks the spot of giggles galore,
With maps made of candy, and jokes at the core.

Seagulls are squawking with witty quips,
As we navigate through these laughter trips.
With every dip from gusts that we face,
We find comedy's treasure in every place.

Here on the sea, with splashes and sparks,
We steer our course, sailing past sharks.
Toward horizons painted with silly design,
In the vastness, our laughter will shine.

The Forgotten Path of Choices

A fork in the road, what a bizarre feat,
One path leads to cake, the other—defeat!
With maps that scribble and arrows that play,
We wander in circles, lost in the fray.

A signpost wobbles; it giggles and mocks,
Pointing to places where nobody talks.
One way is simple, the other a maze,
With silliness lurking in the fog's hazy gaze.

Jellybean flowers grow wild and spry,
Petals giggling like they're flying high.
With every step taken, a chuckle unfolds,
At the choices we make, all whimsically bold.

So here we stroll, with shoes mismatched,
Through paths of laughter that fate has dispatched.
For in choices forgotten, we find the delight,
In a dance through the whims of the night.

Reflections in Glass and Time

In windows wide, we see our fate,
A dance of jokes that won't abate.
Mirrors giggle with a twist,
As time ticks on, it can't be missed.

Framed photos laugh, they wave hello,
Each glance a grin, a comical show.
Chronicles trapped in frames of cheer,
Whisper secrets for those who hear.

The clock strikes funny, hands in a race,
Ticking to rhythms, a laughing pace.
With every second, we chuckle more,
Memory's prank—a mischievous score.

So raise a glass to moments past,
In this time-bound jest, hold it fast.
For in the shimmer of laughter's sheen,
We find our joy in the now unseen.

The Garden of Yesterdays

In bloom, the flowers tell their tales,
With petals bright and cheeky gales.
Each blossom shares a silly spin,
Comedic whispers where dreams begin.

The vegetables poke out, they tease,
Carrots grin with leafy ease.
Tomatoes wobble as they sway,
In this garden bright, come laugh and play.

Bees buzz jokes of nectar bliss,
While dancing on the petals' kiss.
A dish of laughter serves us all,
In laughter's garden, hear the call.

With each ripe fruit, a pun unfolds,
In sunshine's warmth, the humor molds.
As memories sprout beneath the sun,
This garden's laughter weighs a ton.

Echoes Beneath a Starlit Sky

Stars giggle softly, a twinkling cheer,
Blushing bright, as we draw near.
Moonbeams tickle with their glow,
Whispering secrets of a cosmic show.

The night air hums a funny tune,
With shadows dancing beneath the moon.
Crickets chirp their clever jest,
In nature's humor, we're truly blessed.

Each star above has jokes to share,
In constellations, a cosmic pair.
A wish on a dandelion's flight,
Laughs back at us in the still of night.

The universe chuckles, draws us in,
In laughter's embrace, where dreams begin.
So gaze above with a willing heart,
And find the funny in every starry part.

Footprints in Tomorrow's Sand

In grains that shift, we tread with glee,
Each footprint tells where we might be.
Tomorrow's path is drawn in jest,
A sandy trail where folly rests.

Waves roll in, they tease our shoes,
With ticklish splashes, we can't refuse.
Each splash a giggle, each droplet bright,
Runs away with tickles of delight.

Seagulls squawk in comic flight,
Cartwheeling through the ocean's light.
They steal our snacks, then laugh with grace,
In this sticky mess, we find our place.

So dance upon the beach's edge,
With each step, take a silly pledge.
For every grain that slips away,
Holds laughter's echoes, come what may.

Searching for Tomorrow's Light

In a house with socks dated back to noon,
The cat plays chess with a cartoon raccoon.
Dust bunnies dance like they're on a spree,
While I find tomorrow hiding behind a tree.

The fridge hums secrets of old pizza pies,
And the clock just chuckles, it's in on the lies.
Every door creaks with a giggle so sweet,
As I trip over shoes that vanished my feet.

Tides of Time in an Empty Room

In a room where time flows like a gooey jam,
Photos laugh, 'Look, we caught that old clam!'
The chair whispers tales of long-lost meals,
While the curtains peek in for rib-tickling deals.

A vacuum cleaner sings its tired old song,
While the bed claims, 'I'm the one who's been wronged!'

Echoes of footsteps are quick to insist,
That nothing is real and yet all exists.

Beneath the Weight of Creaking Beams

Creaking beams share a laugh, oh what a sight,
As they argue about which ghost has more bite.
Cobwebs knit sweaters for spiders at play,
While my shoes debate if they'll leave today.

The ceiling fan spins tales of forgotten plots,
And the calendar mocks how I forgot my thoughts.
In this circus of chaos, I lose all my haste,
For who knew tomorrow could taste like old paste?

The Last Breath of Yesteryear

Old chairs croak tales of their glory days,
While the wallpaper giggles in tacky displays.
I sip on cold tea with a slice of old bread,
And ponder the dreams of a sock that's misled.

The light bulb flickers with glamorous flair,
It knows all my secrets and won't even care.
Yesterday winks, says, 'I'm still around,'
But today just laughs, making silly sounds.

The Watcher at Daybreak

At dawn, the cat makes plans,
With grand schemes like a wise old man.
He stretches wide, takes one last nap,
Dreams of fish caught in a big, bold trap.

Birds chirp tales of time gone past,
But each worm knows its fate won't last.
The sun sneaks up with a yawning grin,
Ready to see mischief with a spin.

Grass blades whisper secrets low,
While ants debate where to go.
The world awakens, laughter anew,
Chasing shadows, a silly crew.

So let the day begin with cheer,
For what tomorrow holds, we can't steer.
We'll laugh and dance, come what may,
In the antics of dawn's bright display.

Fables of an Unwritten Future

In a land where socks go to roam,
There lies a place we call our home.
Those missing pairs scheme with delight,
Plotting adventures in the night.

The toaster wishes it could fly,
While the fridge sings a lullaby.
Curling up in the echoing hum,
Dreaming of bread, oh, so succulent.

A calendar flips with a wink,
Days fade fast, quicker than you think.
Each scribbled note, a wish untold,
In stories of laughter, bright and bold.

As the moon shines on our silly fight,
We dance around with pure delight.
The future's wild, a page unturned,
Filled with fables long yearned and burned.

Threads of Destiny Intertwined

Weaving pathways of carefree dreams,
Amongst the quirk of life it seems.
Future tangled in a silly dance,
With every twist, a brand new chance.

Colors clash, a rainbow's plight,
As mismatched socks find love at night.
Their stories knit in playful cheer,
Stitching laughter, year after year.

A wandering spoon seeks its mate,
In this kitchen, oh what a fate!
While forks get jealous of the fame,
Of spoons who outshine in the game.

Welcome chaos, come and stay,
In this patchwork of fun at play.
Destiny's threads, a jumbled art,
Woven brightly, sets us apart.

Lanterns in the Mist of Change

As lanterns flicker in morning haze,
They giggle softly, lost in a craze.
Change tiptoes in like a funny clown,
Spinning stories of up and down.

The old clock chuckles in every tick,
Time seems slower when life's a trick.
With each tick-tock, the silliness drops,
Life's a circus, untamed and nonstop.

Puppies roll in a mix of mud,
While the rain clouds form a friendly flood.
Jumping puddles, an uproarious cheer,
In moments like these, worry won't steer.

So let the lanterns light your way,
In the mist where laughter holds sway.
Embrace the change, with joy that swells,
For life's an adventure, with tales to tell.

A Diary of Unfolding Moments

In a room where socks have fun,
They dance when they think no one's around.
The cat joins in, on a lost run,
While clocks spin wild, breaking sound.

Each drawer laughs as it spills out clothes,
A chorus of colors, a joyous sight.
Shadows wiggle and pin their toes,
In this shenanigan of daylight.

The table hums with gossiping plates,
Whispers of crumbs from last night's feast.
They talk of joy, they talk of fates,
And of a cat who thinks it's a beast.

Under the bed, where dust bunnies roam,
They plot adventures, of great delight.
The clock strikes meerkat, time to go home,
To a land where every dream takes flight.

Dreams Whispered Through the Walls

The wall has ears, or so they say,
It giggles when the neighbors shout.
Each brick conceals a game of play,
As whispers of dreams flutter about.

A light bulb buzzes, bright and spry,
It's hosting a party for unseen friends.
The ceiling beams only roll their eye,
As laughter blends, the humor never ends.

Windows frame a scene so absurd,
With dogs in socks, on scooters glide.
The curtains wave, becoming a bird,
They tease the breeze, full of pride.

Hidden behind the wallpaper scene,
A world of jesters and painted fun.
They plot and laugh, wild and serene,
Till the moon arrives, day is done.

Beneath the Cracks in Time

Cracks in the floor like a dance floor bright,
Spiders wear hats, oh what a sight!
They spin in twirls with glimmering threads,
While mice tap dance with chalky spreads.

The air is thick with electric glee,
Shaking with giggles from an unseen mime.
Beneath old rugs where treasures be,
Time hides silly, in playful rhyme.

In corners, echoes of laughter ring,
As dusty footprints trace hilarious trails.
Each creak of the stair adds to the swing,
A symphony where silliness prevails.

Echoes of bedtime stories twist,
As shadows play tag beneath the glow.
Life is a game we can't resist,
In the cracks, imagination flows.

Breathless at the Gates of Change

At dawn, a nascent idea flits,
Chasing the sun with widening eyes.
With painted wings, the concept sits,
Ready to leap into bright blue skies.

The wardrobe sighs, bursting with clothes,
Tangled in laughter, color, and fun.
A parade erupts, it overflows,
With socks and hats enjoying the run.

A plant on the sill can't contain its glee,
Swaying and wriggling with every breeze.
It dreams of dance, oh what a spree,
While sipping sun, with leafy ease.

As change knocks gently at the door,
It tickles the fancy, a playful jest.
Ready or not, here comes the score,
Life's a little laughter, a crazy quest.

A Hearth of Hopes and Fears

In a little shack where dreams collide,
Light dances on walls, a silly guide.
The cat wears a hat, he claims he's wise,
While the toaster toasts bread, plotting surprise.

The clock strikes two, it chimes a tune,
The fridge hums loudly, a hungry croon.
Dishes are laughing, they pop and clunk,
Rivalry's brewing; it smells like punk.

The floorboards creak with tales untold,
As dust bunnies gather; they're bold and old.
A chair winks at walls, so absurdly bright,
It spins stories until the deep night.

Yet here in the chaos, we all take a seat,
In this silly abode, life's laugh is sweet.
With hopes that ignite and fears that tease,
We cozy up tight, wrapped in our ease.

The Lighter Footsteps of Fate

With shoes untied, fate takes a trip,
Every step cheerfully makes us slip.
A banana peel rolls, it knows what's fun,
As laughter erupts, it's not come undone.

The wind howls softly, it pulls at our hair,
Spinning around, we haven't a care.
A squirrel in shades teases the cat,
While the sun smiles wide, wearing a hat.

Balloons float high, ready to play,
They dance through the clouds, in a silly way.
Chasing our hopes like childish dreams,
Life is more playful than it often seems.

So when fate comes knocking, give it a shout,
From windows and rooftops, let laughter sprout.
With every blunder that makes us squeal,
We embrace the lighter, it's all so surreal.

Portraits of What Lies Ahead

In a garden so wacky, with flowers sprouting,
Gardening gnomes are gossiping, shouting.
"Did you see the sun's new hairstyle today?"
As daisies giggle, their petals sway.

Clouds wear pajamas, drifting so slow,
They dream of adventures no one would know.
While shadows debate who's the best at hide,
In the laughter of light, we all want to bide.

Futures are painted in colors quite bright,
With crayons and giggles, we sketch them in light.
From goofy to grand, we trace every line,
Each splash is a whisper, of fate's grand design.

So here we stand, eager to roam,
With portraits of chuckles that feel like home.
In a world spun with whimsy and cheer,
What lies ahead is something we hold dear.

In the Twilight of Forgotten Dreams

As twilight arrives with a wink and a grin,
Old dreams come back just to take a spin.
A dragon in pajamas ignites a spark,
While the moon's on the corner, gossiping stark.

Dust settles down on half-written lines,
Each word a mystery, as silence whines.
Old teddy bears plan an escape from the shelf,
In this twilight lounge, they're dancing by themselves.

With giggles and flickers, dreams come alive,
An octopus juggles; oh, how we thrive!
As shadows twist tales in the fading light,
In this grand theatre, our heart takes flight.

So let's celebrate, with echoes that gleam,
In twilight's embrace, let us dare to dream.
With laughter as chatter, we'll dance 'til it seams,
In a world where reality bursts at the seams.

Conversations with Future Shadows

In a chair made of whispers, shadows meet,
Discussing the quirks of time on repeat.
They laugh at the past, oh what a jest,
With plans to outsmart fate at their best.

They trade silly secrets, a giggle or two,
A future so bright, but clumsy to view.
One claims he can fly if he leans just right,
But falls upside down into yesterday's night.

A shadow's advice is a riddle wrapped tight,
Contemplating tacos in the broad daylight.
"Do you think beans will be legal," he grins,
As they ponder in circles, all giggles and spins.

They dance on the edge of what's yet to come,
With hopes made of cotton and futures so dumb.
Laughter as currency, joy as their meal,
In a world where they thrive, it's all just a steal.

Fragments of a Dream Unfurling

In the attic of whimsy, dreams take their flight,
On a paper-plane made of next week's delight.
They collide with the laughter of moments unseen,
Creating a symphony silly and keen.

One fragment insists it can fly with great ease,
While another rolls down like a breeze through the trees.
"I'll wear spaghetti as my crown," whispers one,
As they giggle and twirl in an endless pun run.

Balloons that speak Spanish float up into space,
While clouds join the fun in a butterfly race.
They cartwheel through midnight with twinkles and glee,
In fragments that dance like a wild jubilee.

Tick-tock goes the clock, full of jokes on repeat,
With punchlines that echo through time's funny seat.
Each dream that unravels, a chuckle bestowed,
As they skip through the years on a bright, winding road.

A Canvas of Unwritten Tomorrows

With paint made of giggles, each stroke brings a grin,
Creating a landscape where nonsense begins.
Clouds shaped like cats frolic over this sphere,
While rabbits in top hats sip tea with no fear.

Tomorrow's a canvas, absurd and surreal,
Where penguins wear bow ties and spin on a wheel.
They barter in riddles, trade laughs for a ride,
In a carnival world where all fun cannot hide.

A jellybean sky swirls with colors so bright,
While unicorns dance 'neath a lantern-lit night.
They juggle their futures, all tangled and bright,
As the painters of laughter welcome in the light.

Each color a promise of joy yet to come,
In this silly adventure on a drum but no drum.
Unwritten tomorrows, a whimsy parade,
A canvas of laughter where dreams never fade.

Keys to the Unseen

In pockets of laughter, the keys jingle bright,
To doors of the future that dance in the night.
A squirrel in a tuxedo holds one with a smirk,
Claiming it opens the kingdom of quirk.

They turn keys of giggles that stay out too late,
Unlocking the doors with a wink and a fate.
"Why did the chicken cross over?" asks the hare,
"To find eggs that giggle and dance in midair!"

With each twist and turn, they fill up the air,
With whispers of nonsense, and humor to spare.
A parade of delight fills the streets as they go,
While unlocks tumble forth, like a whimsical show.

Keys to the unseen, a treasure so rare,
They open to joy and the warmth that we share.
Turning locks in our hearts with each twist of a grin,
Tomorrow's a treasure; let the laughter begin!

Flickering Ghosts of What Could Be

In the attic, old ideas wait,
Dusty dreams on a creaky crate.
A ghost in glasses reads my mind,
Scribbled thoughts lost, hard to find.

A toaster toaster's my best friend,
Burnt toast jokes never seem to end.
Whispers of futures full of cheer,
Like pizza crusts that disappear.

Quirky shadows dance on the wall,
Making up games, I'm having a ball!
They trip on carpets, tumble and sway,
Inventing new ways to brighten my day.

Through the window, tomorrow peeks,
With a grin and a wink, it cheekily sneaks.
Who knew the today was just a jest?
Flickering ghosts, giving life their best!

Between the Pages of Time

In a book where time takes a nap,
Rabbits wear hats—what a funny trap!
Each chapter teases with goofy plots,
Plot twists revealed by tea-stained spots.

The author's pen slips on a whim,
Dropping in gags that make me grin.
A cat who can dance, a dog who can rhyme,
Together they stumble to their prime.

I flip through futures far and wide,
Where laundry spins in a silly ride.
Every page filled with laughter and fun,
Tickling toes until day is done.

Caught in a story, oh what a joke!
Plotting to turn me into a bloke.
Between these pages, time goes awry,
Launching my thoughts into the sky!

The Last Light of Dusk

As the sun bows down, curtains of gold,
A frog in a tuxedo, oh so bold!
He croaks a greeting to the moonlit throng,
And plays the piano to the twilight song.

Chasing shadows that play peek-a-boo,
Whimsical whispers float, maybe two.
A fridge hums loudly with secrets to tell,
While curtains chuckle, all's going well.

Dusk twirls like a dancer on toes,
With each twinkle and wink, mischief grows.
The last light of day brings silliness near,
A symphony of laughter is what we hear.

As stars pop out, like bubbles from a brew,
We sit, we grin, at the show that ensues.
The night rolls in with a cartwheel's delight,
In this twilight dance, everything's alright!

Bridges to Uncharted Realms

In a world where marshmallows float,
I built a bridge with a candy coat.
Swinging on gummy ropes so fine,
I'm off to the realm of pickle brine.

Knobs turned sideways and doors upside down,
Cats in crowns run around town.
Each step is a laugh, each giggle a word,
On this bridge, oh how absurd!

Potato chips shimmer like golden sails,
While bubblegum storms bring gusty gales.
We ride on fish with scuba gear,
In this realm, joy is always near.

Building bridges to places not known,
Where humor and giggles have truly grown.
So come on over, don't hesitate,
Let's dance on the bridge at a whimsical rate!

Whispers from the Horizon

In a place where laughter swells,
Silly stories that time tells,
Jars of pickles dance in rows,
While a chicken wears a rose.

Clouds above with faces grin,
Jumpy squirrels in a spin,
Rainbows made of candy floss,
Where hiccups lead to fun and loss.

A cat that dreams of flying high,
With shoes made just for a pie,
Giggling grass that tickles toes,
In this land where silliness grows.

When the clock strikes twelve, it's true,
Dancing stars say 'Look at you!'
Tomorrow's jests on the way,
Let's make mischief every day!

Shadows of a Future Unseen

In shadows where the giggles hide,
A toaster sings, my silly guide,
Chickens argue who is best,
In the game of feathered zest.

Tomorrow's forecast: laugh and play,
In a world where cats lead the way,
Jumping beans and potato tops,
All dreaming of unending hops.

Dancing ants in tiny suits,
Carrying snacks of wondrous fruits,
Each step brings a joyful squeal,
With belly laughs that never heal.

So in this haze of gleeful trends,
Where logic bends and laughter bends,
We chase the stars and tickle fate,
With a wink that can't be late.

On the Brink of New Dawn

At dawn, the roosters wear cool shades,
While pancake rain falls in cascades,
Toothpaste rivers flow with cheer,
As squirrels sing and sip their beer.

The sun peeks in with a bright grin,
Telling all to let chaos begin,
A blimp that's shaped just like a pie,
Floats by with sprinkles in the sky.

Dancing socks upon the floor,
With every step, they laugh and roar,
A pancake plot twists on the grill,
Where laughter serves as the main thrill.

So let's invite the quirky crew,
Silly dreams all bright and new,
On the brink of wacky sight,
We'll dance till stars burst into light!

Dreams on the Cliff's Edge

On the cliff where breezes sing,
A weasel wears a sparkling ring,
Dreams take flight on lollipop wings,
As the dancing sun joyfully springs.

A trampoline held up by belief,
Jumps through candy, laughs, and grief,
Every bounce brings new delight,
In the chaos of a quirky night.

Octopuses play the guitar,
While moonbeams swim in a jar,
With fish that wear delightful shoes,
Chasing stars, it's hard to lose.

So gather round where dreams are spun,
On the edge where all is fun,
In a world where humor sways,
We'll frolic through eternal plays!

Revelations on a Worn-Out Path

On a path where mysteries twine,
I stumbled upon a strange design.
With slippers askew, my hair a mess,
   The owls hooted, 'Life's a jest!'

In the hedges, whispers sang,
Of ghosts who danced and sometimes rang.
I joined their jig, fell on my face,
   Laughed aloud at my wild chase.

The sun peeked through, a cheeky grin,
As I tripped on roots, lost my skin.
Slack-jawed thoughts of time unfurled,
   What if squirrels ruled this world?

With high hopes and socks mismatched,
I pondered adventures poorly hatched.
Yet in this laugh, confusion bloomed,
   Beneath the wobbly path, I zoomed.

The Gaze of Stars Through the Attic

In an attic filled with dusty dreams,
I battled shadows, or so it seems.
A box of trinkets, no treasure found,
Except for thoughts that danced around.

Old photographs that started to grin,
Combed through memory's thick, wild din.
A star peered in, with a twinkle so bright,
'Your socks don't match, but that's all right!'

I chuckled back, as dust motes spun,
Each twirl a story, each laugh a pun.
A telescope aimed at the wildest sights,
Yet I just saw my own misplaced nights.

In that space where secrets lay,
I found a way to joke and play.
Among the stars, I skipped and hopped,
Wondering when the laughter stopped.

A Journey Beyond the Final Instant

Off I went with a skip and sway,
To the land where yesterday turned to play.
My compass spun, with a cheeky wink,
While I pondered if cows really blink.

A rabbit shouted, 'Time is a trick!'
As I slipped on quotes, scripted quick.
We danced through moments, hid in laughs,
Counting the days, and my other halves.

Every leap was a puzzling thrill,
With clocks that giggled, refusing to stand still.
Fuzzy creatures chatted in bits,
While echoes of nonsense filled the skits.

At each turn, there whispered fate,
Who knew I'd say, 'Are we there—wait?'
So off again, with silly schemes,
Where yesterday meets tomorrow's dreams.

The Pulse of Tomorrow's Wishes

In a quirky realm where wishes spun,
I found a clock that weighed a ton.
Tick-tock giggles from gears of gold,
Said dreams aren't shy—they're just bold.

With every tick—a horse flew by,
Claiming he'd teach a swift way to fly.
I hopped on board; we rode through time,
While I wondered if this was a crime.

The trees wore hats, the rivers grinned,
A smiling sun as my trusty friend.
Every wish whispered, 'Come and play!'
We danced on clouds in a giggly sway.

But as we laughed, the sun kissed night,
Leaving me with a funny fright.
For as time ticks, life's pulse remains,
In a world where wishes have no chains.

A Threshold to Infinity

A door squeaked loud, a cat fell flat,
With socks mismatched, and a hat so daft.
Time slips away, a clock starts to spin,
I trip on my laces, the fun's about to begin.

Jumping through walls, or so I might claim,
The fridge light flickers, it's playing a game.
Lost in the pantry, where snacks often hide,
Who knew granola bars would take me for a ride?

Dreams full of jellybeans and endless pie,
As I dance with the shadows that flutter and fly.
A tumble through space, with a giggle or two,
In a world where nonsense is always the cue.

So here's to the moments that tickle our souls,
Where laughter transforms into wild, jolly goals.
With each funny stumble, and goofy mistake,
Life's sweet absurdities are ours to partake.

Secrets Beneath the Gnarled Oak

Under a tree that whispers and creaks,
Lies an old treasure where laughter sneaks.
Squirrels with secrets, and nuts stacked so high,
They chatter and scold, with a glint in their eye.

A picnic blanket, a feast fit for kings,
With sandwiches dancing, and cakes with wings.
A hesitant bite revealed a strange taste,
Was that ketchup or jam? I just couldn't waste!

The shadows around us, they wiggle and sway,
As lights bounce off branches and join in the play.
We plays tag with the breeze, it shrieks with delight,
Under gnarled oak limbs, we frolic till night.

The laughter will echo as memories grow,
In the heart of the forest, where whimsy will flow.
Secrets uncovered in the most silly ways,
In a dance with the trees, we'll laugh through our days.

Light Cascading Through the Void

A light switch flickers in a realm upside down,
Where shadows wear slippers and frown on the clown.
Floating through colors like jelly, so bright,
The universe chuckles; it's a wobbly sight.

Stars are a giggle, they twinkle and tease,
As planets spin stories on whimsy's cool breeze.
Cosmic friends laughing in faraway places,
While comets do cartwheels, pulling funny faces.

In the void where the echoes of nonsense all play,
Time trips on laughter; it's a grand cabaret.
With each twirling thought, we try not to blink,
For fear we'll miss magic in the space of the ink.

So gather the sparkles that shimmy and glide,
As joy dances wildly with no need to hide.
In light's funny prism, we take a grand flight,
Cascading through laughter brings dreams into sight.

Gaze of the Distant Dawn

Morning yawns wide with a tangled-up hue,
Chasing after dreams in a warm cup of brew.
Whispers of morning, they tickle my ear,
As the sunlight spills giggles, brightening near.

The rooster's off-key, he's singing a tune,
A symphony built on a very silly rune.
As the horizon blushes, putting on a show,
The clouds throw confetti, saying, 'Here we go!'

With pancake stacks wobbling, syrup so sweet,
A dance party starts on my breakfast plate seat.
I slip on some butter, the floor starts to spin,
But laughter's my anchor; I know I'll win.

So face the new dawn with a wink and a smile,
Let the world start laughing; we'll go the extra mile.
In the gaze of the morning, adventure's in sight,
With each silly moment, the day feels so right.

Echoes of a Day Yet to Come

Beneath the ceiling, shadows play,
As sleepy cats claim the new day.
Ticking clocks in a comedic race,
While socks vanish, a silly chase.

Chairs that creak in laughter's tune,
A broom that dances, quite the boon.
Tomorrow waits with a quirky grin,
As dust bunnies invite you in.

A robot vacuum slips on the floor,
And trip over the cat—oh, what a score!
Each doorway laughs as you try to squeeze,
A reminder that chaos is life's expertise.

In this strange corner where dreams collide,
Time winks cheekily, full of pride.
With giggles echoing all around,
Tomorrow's antics waiting to be found.

Foundations of Forgotten Futures

Foundations built on wobbly dreams,
Where jellybeans flow like bubbling streams.
Walls of laughter, ceilings of cheer,
Each corner sings, 'Come over here!'

A fridge that spins tales of late-night snacks,
Cabbage that dances on the old knickknacks.
In rooms of echoes, just hold your hat,
Watch out for the jumping, laughing cat!

Prancing shadows flit across the floor,
A dancing mop that twirls and swore.
Tomorrow whispers silly schemes,
In this abode of whimsical dreams.

Under the stairs, a pirate's tale,
With hidden treasure on a rubber snail.
Futures forgotten but filled with glee,
Cheers to tomorrow, come join the spree!

Time's Lament in an Abandoned Hall

In the great hall, time sneezes loud,
Dust clouds forming a playful shroud.
Chairs all gather for a gossip fest,
While lazy ghosts put gossip to the test.

Windows wide, don't mind the drafts,
As silliness trails in clockwork drafts.
The chandelier hums a tuneless song,
While curtains tease with a playful throng.

Echoes bounce off the forgotten wall,
Where memory prances like a basketball.
In the silence, laughter creeps,
Dancing dust flings itself in heaps.

Time laments, but in jest not grief,
In a hall where mirth wears a leaf.
With echoes ready to tickle your toes,
Tomorrow tumbles in revealing its prose.

Windows to What Might Be

Through the windows, peeks a grin,
Silly scenes where nightmares begin.
A world where toast plays hide and seek,
And teapots cheer as they spill their peak.

Hats on hats, a fashionable joke,
While shoes chat as though they spoke.
Windows wide to wonders unclear,
With laughter ringing for all to hear.

The sky's a canvas, splashed and bright,
Where pajamas dance in the broad daylight.
Time laughs and twirls a clever twist,
With every minute that you dare to miss.

What might be just around the bend,
Is a party waiting for you, my friend.
So take a peek through the fantastical view,
In tomorrow's theater, there's room for you!

Vows of Time Beneath the Eaves

In a creaky old nook, time plays peek-a-boo,
Whispers of laughter float where the shadows grew.
Chairs made for sitting, yet stacked for a joke,
Soon the roof might surrender, let loose all the smoke.

The clock ticks in circles, with hands made of cheese,
It giggles and twerks, oh how it aims to please!
Beneath the broad eaves, surprises collide,
With time taking vows, we all take a ride.

Potions and puddles just waiting to spill,
Who knew a spilled drink could give such a thrill?
Between sips of laughter, the moments expand,
With echoes of chuckles, we dance on hot sand.

In this quirky old spot where the future is free,
Every falter in steps is a chance to agree.
So toast to the whims that tomorrow can send,
For time here is funny, and the laughter won't end.

Cloaked in the Mist of Possibility

Wrapped up in clouds where the silly winds flow,
Dreams tiptoe sideways and giggle they show.
In a mist of mischief that tickles the air,
Possibilities prance in their polka-dot wear.

What's that? A promise scribbled in chalk?
Hopping on toasters, they stroll and they talk.
The moon tells a secret, the stars roll their eyes,
As shadows throw parties, oh what a surprise!

These jokes of existence float gently on puffs,
As we dance with the quirks, in laughter we huff.
Swirling in mists that bend time like a straw,
Each moment's a punchline, and oh, what a flaw!

With giggles and chuckles as our compass we steer,
What's cloaked in the mist brings a waddle of cheer.
So let's toast to tomorrow, with whimsy we play,
In a world where the funny just dances away.

Ancestral Echoes in the Air

Down the corridor, whispers frolic and sneak,
Ancestors chuckle, their humor unique.
Knitting their tales with a wink and a grin,
Gossiping softly, where do we begin?

In portraits they dangle, but watch where they sway,
One wink from a cousin, now how will we play?
Voices in echoes, a ruckus from yore,
Suggesting our history's a never-ending store.

A great-aunt in petticoats, dynamically bold,
Plays jacks with the shadows, her laughter retold.
Tripping on tales that defy all the rules,
Ancestral jokes wrapped in old dusty tools.

So bring out the punchlines from deep in the grove,
Where dimensions collide, and humor can rove.
With giggles as lanterns, we stumble through layers,
In echoes of laughter, our past becomes players.

Dances with Tomorrow's Uncertainty

Tiptoeing forward, where future's a dance,
With wobbling partners who twirl in a trance.
The floorboards are creaking, the rhythm's a mess,
As we boogie with fate in a comic recess.

Yesterday's frazzle we toss in a spin,
Flipping the now, oh, where do we begin?
With feet made of rubber, the laughter ignites,
Each hop brings a giggle, twinkling through nights.

Uncertain tomorrow, dressed wild in surprise,
Waltzing with mishaps right before our eyes.
Who knows what the future has hidden in store?
A rave or a tumble, or maybe a snore?

So let's salsa with chaos, embrace the unknown,
In dances of whimsy, together we've grown.
The steps of tomorrow, forever we'll trot,
With joy on our faces, we stumble, but not!

Nightfall on the Edge of Change

At dusk, the cat wore pants,
Ready for its evening dance.
The fish dived into the ground,
In laughter, joy will abound.

The moon played hide-and-seek,
While chairs began to speak.
A dog with a purple hat,
Wagged his tail, 'Isn't that fat?'

Balloons floated in the air,
Singing tunes without a care.
The clocks decided to nap,
Creating chaos on the map.

As stars began to giggle bright,
A mouse took flight into the night.
With each tick, the world swayed,
In this funny masquerade.

Canvas of the Unseen

The walls are stuck in indecision,
Painting dreams with precision.
A goat decided to make art,
Crafting it from pure heart.

Colors danced on the ceiling,
While the floor had a feeling.
Chairs wore slippers, took a stroll,
Chasing crumbs and a bread roll.

The laughter echoed, doors would sway,
As shadows pranked the light of day.
A rabbit with a paintbrush drawn,
Created puns from dusk till dawn.

Yet here they stood in hues so bright,
Creating smiles with sheer delight.
On this canvas, the unseen sings,
Of everything that funny brings.

Paradoxes Sculpted in Dust

In a dusty room, a vacuum swayed,
Beneath it, laughter played.
An umbrella opened with a spin,
As rain began to fall within.

A cactus wore a hat so fine,
Declaring, 'Oh, this day is mine!'
The windows giggled as they creaked,
While shadows danced, the lights retreated.

Books took flight, a whirlwind twirl,
Creating storms in a paper world.
Dust bunnies plotted to take a ride,
While clocks joked of time with pride.

Yet in this paradoxical space,
Laughter lingered, leaving trace.
For in the dust, we find our muse,
And perhaps, more than we could use.

Serendipity in the Shadows

In the shadows, whispers smirk,
As kittens with spectacles go to work.
Chasing dreams and shiny things,
On teacups, all their laughter rings.

A broom took wing, a dance of finesse,
While shovels played at true success.
Cobwebs rejoiced in the moon's embrace,
As fame found the tiniest space.

Pies floated by, on a sugar breeze,
While shadows played a game of tease.
A mirror cracked, but laughed instead,
Reflecting joy, not dread.

Serendipity reigned supreme,
In this wacky, wondrous dream.
For in the shadows, fun does grow,
Embracing all who dare to know.

Lanterns of Hope in the Gloom

In a room full of shadows, a lantern's aglow,
Three squirrels dance chaotically, putting on a show.
Their acorn hats wobble, they trip on the floor,
While the cat in the corner just demands an encore.

The walls are all leaning, a laugh or a sigh,
As ghosts try to juggle, they're quite the sly guy.
With a wink and a nudge, they fall for the trick,
Who knew that a poltergeist could be so quick?

A toaster keeps popping, not sure why it's brown,
It wanted to be a chef, now it's just a clown.
The fridge hums a tune, and the kettle joins in,
Together they band in a kitcheny din.

So here in the gloom, with laughter and cheer,
An odd little family is always near.
With lanterns of hope lighting shadows so wide,
This quirky abode is where joy cannot hide.

The Promise of a Coming Dawn

When night tries to linger, the sun plays a game,
A waltz with the clouds, never quite the same.
With each silly tumble the stars all cheer loud,
And the moon rolls his eyes, trapped under a shroud.

Watch the rooster perform, he thinks he's a star,
But forgets it's a nap time, he lies where we are.
The sun peeks around, he giggles and beams,
Planning his entrance, bursting forth with dreams.

In a flock full of sheep, one dares to be bold,
It paints itself yellow, and acts quite controlled.
The others just bleat, they look all bemused,
At this quirky vision that has them confused.

Yet every dawn whispers, "Let's give it a go,"
For life is a circus, with much more to show.
With promise and laughter, the daylight breaks free,
To twirl in the air, unbound as can be.

Tales of Light in Dark Corners

In shadows that shiver, a tale comes to light,
Where dust bunnies plot their heroic delight.
A lamp standing tall becomes valiant and wise,
As moths rally round, with excitement in their eyes.

There once was a closet, quite secretive too,
With socks in a standoff, unsure what to do.
But a rogue little shoe, in a twist of fate,
Decided to leap, "Let's dance, not debate!"

A broom in the corner longed for a ball,
While a dustpan sighed, "Can't we all just haul?"
Yet with every twirl, the room starts to quake,
A flash of pure joy, and the floorboards can shake.

So gather your laughter, in dark corners near,
There's magic in chaos, you need not fear.
With tales of pure light that play hide and seek,
Find joy in the mess, let your heart learn to speak.

Map of Where Dreams Collide

There's a map on the wall, it's wrinkled and torn,
Marked with bizarre dreams, like a patchwork of corn.
A unicorn signals, "This way to the fun!"
While teapots spill tea, blending adventures as one.

A snail with a compass, slow but so grand,
Embarks on a journey across "Sillyland."
When clouds turn to candy, they stretch for a taste,
And giggles erupt at this sweet little haste.

At intersections of laughter, the paths intertwine,
With bubbles as signs, all sparkly and fine.
A rubber duck flotilla sails past with a cheer,
Saying "Join the parade, there's no room for fear!"

So trust in the map, where your wild dreams reside,
In a world full of laughter, let joy be your guide.
When dreams start to merge, let your heart find the way,
In this whimsical realm, let your spirit play.